PIANO | VOCAL | GUITAR • CD   **VOLUME 125**

HAL•LEONARD

Piano Play-Along

KATY PERRY

PAGE	TITLE	DEMO TRACK	PLAY-ALONG TRACK
2	California Gurls	1	9
16	Firework	2	10
9	Hot N Cold	3	11
22	I Kissed a Girl	4	12
26	Last Friday Night (T.G.I.F.)	5	13
32	Part of Me	6	14
44	Teenage Dream	7	15
38	Wide Awake	8	16

Cover photo: JAKE BAILEY/AUGUST

ISBN 978-1-4768-6876-9

HAL•LEONARD®
CORPORATION
7777 W. BLUEMOUND RD. P.O. BOX 13819 MILWAUKEE, WI 53213

In Australia Contact:
Hal Leonard Australia Pty. Ltd.
4 Lentara Court
Cheltenham, Victoria, 3192 Australia
Email: ausadmin@halleonard.com.au

Visit Hal Leonard Online at
www.halleonard.com

CALIFORNIA GURLS

Words and Music by KATY PERRY,
BONNIE McKEE, LUKASZ GOTTWALD,
MAX MARTIN, BENJAMIN LEVIN,
CALVIN BROADUS, MIKE LOVE
and BRIAN WILSON

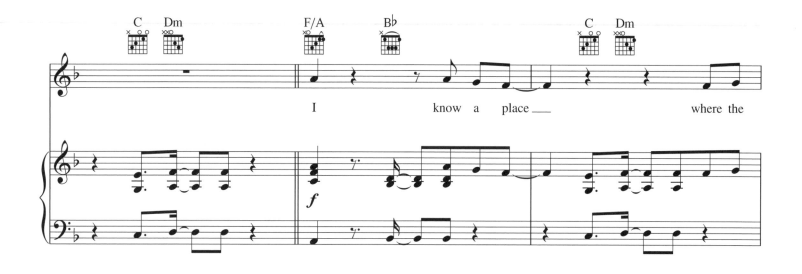

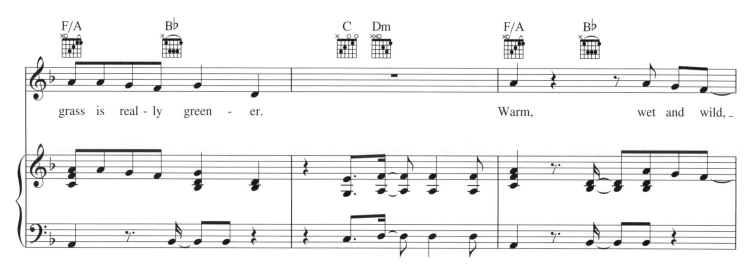

HOT N COLD

Words and Music by KATY PERRY,
MAX MARTIN and LUKASZ GOTTWALD

With energy

You change your mind ___ like a girl ___ chang-es clothes. ___
We used to be ___ just like twins, ___ so in sync. ___

Yeah, you P. M. S. ___ like a bitch, ___
The same en-er-gy ___ now's a dead ___

I would know. ___ And you al-ways think, ___
bat-ter-y. ___ Used to laugh ___ 'bout noth-ing, ___

FIREWORK

Words and Music by KATY PERRY,
MIKKEL ERIKSEN, TOR ERIK HERMANSEN,
ESTHER DEAN and SANDY WILHELM

Dance Pop

I KISSED A GIRL

Words and Music by KATY PERRY,
CATHY DENNIS, MAX MARTIN
and LUKASZ GOTTWALD

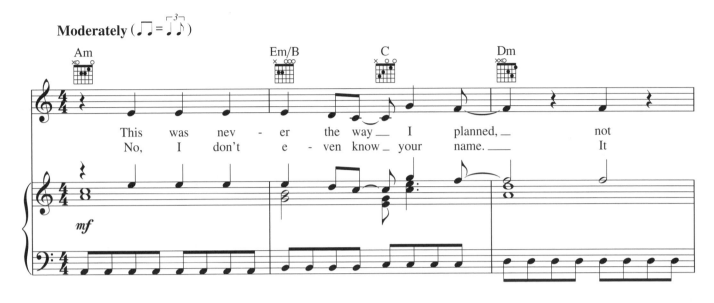

This was nev-er the way I planned, not
No, I don't e-ven know your name.

my in-ten- tion. I got so brave, drink in hand,
does-n't mat- ter. You're my ex- per- i- men- tal game,

lost my dis-cre- tion. It's not what
just hu- man na- ture. It's not what

LAST FRIDAY NIGHT
(T.G.I.F.)

Words and Music by KATY PERRY,
BONNIE McKEE, LUKASZ GOTTWALD,
MAX MARTIN and BENJAMIN LEVIN

* Recorded a half step higher.

PART OF ME

Words and Music by KATY PERRY,
LUKASZ GOTTWALD, MAX MARTIN
and BONNIE McKEE

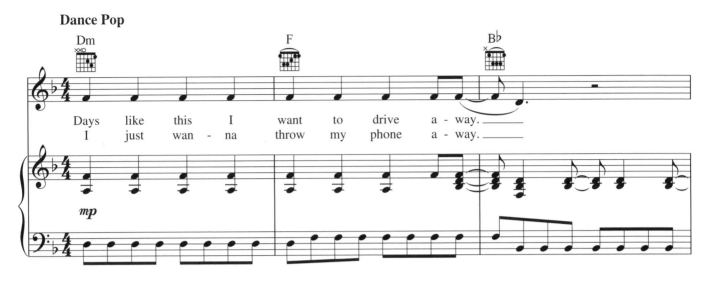

Days like this I want to drive a-way.
I just wan-na throw my phone a-way.

Pack my bags and watch your shad-ow fade.
Find out who is real-ly there for me.

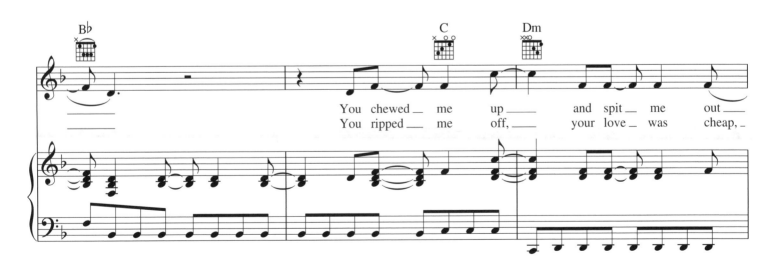

You chewed me up and spit me out
You ripped me off, your love was cheap,

*2nd time

WIDE AWAKE

Words and Music by KATY PERRY,
LUKASZ GOTTWALD, MAX MARTIN,
HENRY WALTER and BONNIE McKEE

TEENAGE DREAM

Words and Music by KATY PERRY,
BONNIE McKEE, LUKASZ GOTTWALD,
MAX MARTIN and BENJAMIN LEVIN

THE ULTIMATE SONGBOOKS

HAL•LEONARD
PIANO PLAY-ALONG

These great songbook/CD packs come with our standard arrangements for piano and voice with guitar chord frames plus a CD.

The CD includes a full performance of each song, as well as a second track without the piano part so you can play "lead" with the band! Volumes 86 and beyond also include the Amazing Slow Downer technology so PC and Mac users can adjust the recording to any tempo without changing the pitch!

HAL•LEONARD®
CORPORATION
7777 W. BLUEMOUND RD. P.O. BOX 13819
MILWAUKEE, WISCONSIN 53213

Visit Hal Leonard Online at
www.halleonard.com

0313

PIANO PLAY-ALONG

Each volume in this series comes with
a CD of orchestrated arrangements.
The music in this book matches these
recorded orchestrations. There are two
tracks for each—a full performance for
listening, plus a separate backing track
which lets you be the soloist! The
music even includes a separate vocal
staff, plus guitar frames, so you or your
friends can also sing or strum along!

The CD is playable on any CD player, and
is also enhanced so Mac and PC users can
adjust the recording to any tempo without
changing the pitch!

California Gurls

Firework

Hot N Cold

I Kissed a Girl

Last Friday Night (T.G.I.F.)

Part of Me

Teenage Dream

Wide Awake

Book $6.99, CD $8.00 = **Pkg U.S. $14.99**
Parts not sold separately

8 84088 79288 6

HL00109373

EXCLUSIVELY DISTRIBUTED BY
HAL•LEONARD®

ISBN 978-1-4768-6876-9

9 781476 868769